EXTREME

P R
P
PLANTS

Anita Ganeri

Raintree

www.raintreepublishers.co.uk
Visit our website to find out more information about Raintree books.

To order:
☎ Phone 0845 6044371
🖶 Fax +44 (0) 1865 312263
🖥 Email myorders@raintreepublishers.co.uk

Customers from outside the UK please telephone +44 1865 312262

Raintree is an imprint of Capstone Global Library Limited, a company incorporated in England and Wales having its registered office at 7 Pilgrim Street, London, EC4V 6LB – Registered company number: 6695582

Text © Capstone Global Library Limited 2013
First published in hardback in 2013
Paperback edition first published in 2014
The moral rights of the proprietor have been asserted.

Edited by Dan Nunn, Rebecca Rissman, and Catherine Veitch
Designed by Cynthia Della-Rovere
Picture research by Tracy Cummins
Production by Alison Parsons
Originated by Capstone Global Library
Printed and bound in China by CTPS

ISBN 978 1 406 23790 0 (hardback)
16 15 14 13 12
10 9 8 7 6 5 4 3 2 1

ISBN 978 1 406 23795 5 (paperback)
17 16 15 14 13
10 9 8 7 6 5 4 3 2 1

British Library Cataloguing in Publication Data
Ganeri, Anita
Peculiar plants. -- (Extreme nature)
581.4-dc22
A full catalogue record for this book is available from the British Library.

Acknowledgements
We would like to thank the following for permission to reproduce photographs: Corbis pp. 4 (© Michael DeFreitas/Robert Harding World Imager), 7 (© Frans Lanting), 11 (© Henry Lehn/Visuals Unlimited), 26 (© Mauricio Handler/National Geographic Society); Getty Images pp. 5 (Martin Harvey), 9 (Altrendo Panoramic), 13 (Coke Whitworth), 16 (David C Tomlinson), 24 (Roger de la Harpe), 25 (China Photos/Stringer); National Geographic Stock p. 6 (FRANS LANTING), 19 (KONRAD WOTHE/ MINDEN PICTURES), 22 (MICHAEL & PATRICIA FOGDEN/ MINDEN PICTURES); Photolibrary pp. 10 (Malcolm Schuyl/FLPA), 15 (Nick Garbutt), 17 (HSchweiger Hschweiger), 18 (Jean-Philippe Delobelle); Shutterstock pp. 8 (© Jorg Hackemann), 12 (© a9photo), 14 (© Calvin Chan), 20 (© hunta), 21 (© gary yim), 23 (© Pichugin Dmitry), 27 (© Heather A. Craig).

Cover photograph of a rafflesia reproduced with permission of Getty Images (Renaud Visage).

Some words are shown in bold, **like this**. You can find out what they mean by looking in the glossary.

Contents

What are peculiar plants?

Did you know that some trees grow taller than skyscrapers? Or that some plants eat mice? Peculiar plants grow all over the world. Some plants are record-breakers. Others have special **features** to help them live in **hostile**, or unfriendly, **habitats**.

mangrove tree

Stone plants look like stones to hide from hungry animals.

Freaky flower

The rafflesia flower grows in the **rainforest** in south-east Asia. It is the world's biggest flower and smells of rotten meat.

rafflesia bud

DID YOU KNOW?
The rafflesia can grow up to one metre across. That's about as wide as your outstretched arms.

Towering tree

A giant sequoia tree, nicknamed the "General Sherman" tree, grows in California, USA. It is as tall as 15 houses and is the biggest tree on Earth.

GENERAL SHERMAN

DID YOU KNOW?

The "General Sherman" contains enough wood to make billions of matchsticks.

Strangler fig

The strangler fig grows in the **rainforest**. Its seed **sprouts** high up on the branch of another tree. Then the roots grow down towards the ground and wrap tightly around the tree. The roots suck up the tree's water supply and the tree dies.

DID YOU KNOW?

The strangler fig was given its name because it strangles other plants to death.

Meat-eating plants

The Venus flytrap plant eats insects in a nasty way. The insect touches some hairs on the plant. This makes the leaf snap shut, trapping the insect. Then the plant makes special juices that turn the insect's body into liquid for the plant to soak up.

Pitcher plants have strange, jug-shaped leaves. Insects land on the leaves, looking for **nectar** to drink. But they slide down into the "jug" and drown in the pool of water inside. Then the plant **digests** them.

The biggest pitcher plant, the Rajah, catches the poo of small animals such as rats and mice.

Prickly plants

Giant saguaro cacti grow in the deserts of the United States and Mexico. They can weigh 10 tonnes. That's as heavy as six large cars!

The cacti store water in their thick stems to use when there is a **drought**.

DID YOU KNOW?

Elf owls make cool nests for themselves inside saguaro cacti.

Bulging baobab

A baobab tree has branches that stick up into the air and look like upside-down roots. They store water in their trunks, which bulge as they fill up.

DID YOU KNOW? There is a **legend** that anyone who picks a baobab flower will be eaten by a lion.

Baobabs mostly grow on the island of Madagascar, off the **coast** of Africa.

Out in the cold

High up on a mountain, it is windy and cold. Mountain plants have special ways to keep warm. The flowers and leaves of edelweiss are covered in furry white hairs to keep it warm.

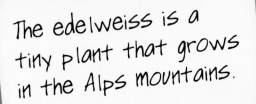

The edelweiss is a tiny plant that grows in the Alps mountains.

Snow **algae** from icy Antarctica have a chemical inside them that stops their bodies from freezing. This algae colours the snow red.

Weird welwitschia

The welwitschia grows in the Namib Desert in Namibia, in Africa. The leaves collect **dew**, which the plant needs to stay alive. The plant has only two leaves. But the leaves get torn to pieces by the wind.

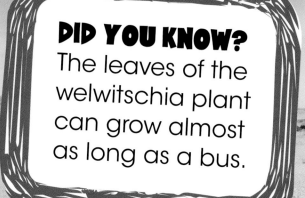

DID YOU KNOW?

The leaves of the welwitschia plant can grow almost as long as a bus.

Giant water lily

Giant water lily leaves float on the Amazon River in South America. Each leaf can grow more than 2 metres wide (the size of a small garden pond).

DID YOU KNOW?

Water lily leaves float because they have spaces filled with air inside them.

Giant water lily leaves are very strong. People can sit on one without sinking!

Super-sized seaweed

Huge seaweed forests grow along the **coast** of California in the United States. This seaweed is called giant kelp. It has ribbon-like stems that can grow over 50 metres long. That is about as long as two swimming pools!

DID YOU KNOW?
A giant kelp stem can grow as tall as an adult person in just four days.

Sea otters live among the stems of giant kelp.

Quiz: What am I?

Read the clues, then try to work out "What am I?". Find the answers at the bottom of page 29. But guess first!

1) I have orange-brown petals.
I smell of rotten meat.
I can grow up to one metre across.
What am I?

2) I grow in the **rainforest**.
I strangle other trees.
I **sprout** on a tree branch.
What am I?

3) I have hairy leaves.

I eat insects.

My name is also a planet.

What am I?

4) I float on a river.

I can be as big as a pond.

I am strong enough to sit on.

What am I?

5) I grow in the desert.

My leaves are as

long as a bus.

I drink **dew**.

What am I?

Glossary

algae plants that often live in water. Seaweed is a type of algae.

coast edge of the land that borders the sea

dew drops of water that form at night on plants and other surfaces

digest change food so that it can be taken into the body

drought time of very dry weather when there is very little or no rain

feature special body part, pattern, or kind of behaviour

habitat place where a plant or an animal lives

hostile difficult to live in; not very friendly or welcoming

legend ancient story that may or may not be true

nectar sweet syrup found deep inside flowers

rainforest forest that is warm and wet all year round

sprout spread out shoots

Find out more

Books

Plants! (*Time for Kids Science Scoops*), Brenda Iasevoli (Harper Trophy, 2006)

The Deadliest Plants on Earth (*The World's Deadliest*), Connie Colwell Miller (Raintree, 2011)

Venus Flytraps, Bladderworts and Other Wild and Amazing Plants (National Geographic Science Chapters series), Monica Halpern (National Geographic Society, 2006)

Websites

www.edenproject.com

This is the website of the Eden Project in Cornwall. The Eden Project has plants from around the world, including a rainforest you can walk through.

www.kew.org

This is the website of the Royal Botanic Gardens at Kew, London, which has a huge collection of peculiar plants from around the world.

Index